Inside the Threat: The Making of the Dirty Bomb and Homeland Security's Fight to Stop It

ROBERTO RODRIGUEZ

2023

Copyright Page

TITLE: Inside the Threat: The Making of the Dirty Bomb and Homeland Security's Fight to Stop It

1ST Edition

Copyright @ 2023

ISBN: 9798223586180

Table of Contents

Inside the Threat: The Making of the Dirty Bomb and Homeland Security's Fight to Stop It

By Roberto Miguel Rodriguez

Chapter 1: Introduction to Dirty Bombs and Homeland Security Efforts

Understanding the Threat of Dirty Bombs

The threat of dirty bombs poses a significant risk to national security and the safety of our citizens. In this subchapter, we will delve into the intricacies of this threat, exploring the various factors involved in the making of a dirty bomb and the efforts undertaken by the Department of Homeland Security to prevent its creation by terrorists.

One of the key aspects to understanding this threat lies in comprehending the various nuclear materials detection and tracking technologies available. As security agents, it is essential to stay updated on the latest advancements in this field to effectively detect and intercept any potential threats.

Additionally, we will explore the security protocols in place for nuclear facilities and transportation. Ensuring the highest level of security for these facilities and transportation routes is crucial in preventing terrorists from acquiring the necessary materials to construct a dirty bomb.

In today's interconnected world, cybersecurity measures are of paramount importance. We will discuss the measures taken to prevent terrorist hacking of nuclear systems, as any breach in these systems could lead to catastrophic consequences.

Furthermore, we will explore radiation detection and monitoring strategies. By understanding these strategies, security agents can effectively identify and mitigate any radiation threats, ensuring a rapid response to potential dirty bomb incidents.

Intelligence gathering on terrorist organizations' interest in dirty bombs is another critical aspect to be addressed. By staying informed on their intentions and capabilities, security agents can proactively disrupt any plans before they come to fruition.

International cooperation and information sharing on nuclear threats are vital in addressing this global threat. We will examine the efforts made to collaborate with international partners to share intelligence and enhance our collective ability to prevent dirty bomb attacks.

Emergency response plans and preparedness for dirty bomb incidents are essential components of any comprehensive security strategy. We will delve into the best practices for developing robust emergency response plans, ensuring a coordinated and swift response in the event of a dirty bomb incident.

Public awareness campaigns play a significant role in preventing dirty bomb attacks. We will discuss the importance of educating the public about the dangers of dirty bombs and promoting vigilance and reporting of suspicious activities.

Legal frameworks and penalties for individuals involved in dirty bomb activities are crucial deterrents. We will explore the existing legal frameworks and the penalties associated with engaging in such activities, emphasizing the consequences for those involved.

Lastly, we will touch upon the ongoing research and development of advanced technologies aimed at enhancing our dirty bomb prevention efforts. Staying at the forefront of technological advancements is crucial to staying one step ahead of potential threats.

In conclusion, understanding the threat of dirty bombs is imperative for security agents. By comprehending the various aspects discussed in this subchapter, we can strengthen our efforts to prevent the creation of dirty bombs by terrorists and ensure the safety and security of our nation and its people.

The Role of the Department of Homeland Security

Introduction:

The Department of Homeland Security (DHS) plays a crucial role in safeguarding the United States from various threats, including the making of a dirty bomb. This subchapter will explore the efforts made by the DHS to prevent terrorists from acquiring and using nuclear materials, as well as the strategies and technologies employed to combat this threat.

Nuclear Materials Detection and Tracking Technologies:

One of the primary responsibilities of the DHS is to develop and implement advanced technologies for detecting and tracking nuclear materials. Through continuous research and development, the DHS aims to enhance the capabilities of its radiation detection systems, ensuring the timely identification of any illicit nuclear activities.

Security Protocols for Nuclear Facilities and Transportation:

To prevent terrorists from gaining access to nuclear materials, the DHS collaborates closely with nuclear facilities and transportation agencies to establish stringent security protocols. This includes thorough background checks for personnel, secure transportation methods, and the implementation of robust physical security measures at nuclear facilities.

Cybersecurity Measures to Prevent Terrorist Hacking:

Recognizing the potential for terrorists to exploit cyber vulnerabilities in nuclear systems, the DHS has prioritized cybersecurity measures. Through continuous monitoring and threat intelligence sharing, the

DHS aims to prevent hackers from gaining unauthorized access to critical nuclear infrastructure.

Radiation Detection and Monitoring Strategies:

The DHS employs comprehensive radiation detection and monitoring strategies to identify any unusual radiation levels. By deploying mobile detection units and utilizing advanced sensors, the DHS can quickly respond to potential dirty bomb threats and mitigate the risks associated with radioactive materials.

Intelligence Gathering on Terrorist Interest in Dirty Bombs:

The DHS actively gathers intelligence on terrorist organizations' interest in dirty bombs. Through intelligence sharing with domestic and international partners, the DHS aims to stay ahead of potential threats and disrupt any activities related to the acquisition or production of a dirty bomb.

International Cooperation and Information Sharing:

Recognizing the global nature of nuclear threats, the DHS fosters international cooperation and information sharing on nuclear threats. By collaborating with foreign counterparts, the DHS can exchange best practices, enhance intelligence sharing, and collectively combat the proliferation of dirty bombs.

Emergency Response Plans and Preparedness:

The DHS develops comprehensive emergency response plans and conducts regular drills to ensure preparedness in the event of a dirty bomb incident. By coordinating with federal, state, and local agencies, the DHS aims to minimize the impact of such an incident and protect public safety.

Public Awareness Campaigns:

The DHS conducts public awareness campaigns to educate the general public about the dangers of dirty bombs. By raising awareness, the DHS aims to empower individuals to report suspicious activities and enhance overall preparedness within communities.

Legal Frameworks and Penalties:

The DHS works closely with law enforcement agencies and lawmakers to establish stringent legal frameworks and penalties for individuals involved in dirty bomb activities. By imposing severe consequences, the DHS aims to deter potential individuals from engaging in such dangerous activities.

Research and Development of Advanced Technologies:

The DHS invests in research and development to enhance dirty bomb prevention efforts. By exploring cutting-edge technologies, such as advanced sensors and detection systems, the DHS strives to stay ahead of evolving threats and continuously improve its capabilities.

Conclusion:

The DHS plays a vital role in preventing the making of a dirty bomb by terrorists. Through robust detection and monitoring technologies, security protocols, intelligence gathering, international cooperation, and public awareness campaigns, the DHS aims to safeguard the nation from this grave threat. By constantly adapting and innovating, the DHS stays at the forefront of efforts to enhance dirty bomb prevention and protect national security.

Chapter 2: Nuclear Materials Detection and Tracking Technologies

Current Technologies for Detecting Nuclear Materials

In the ongoing battle against terrorism and the threat of dirty bombs, the Department of Homeland Security (DHS) has made significant strides in developing and implementing cutting-edge technologies for the detection of nuclear materials. These technologies play a crucial role in safeguarding our nation's security and preventing the catastrophic consequences of a dirty bomb attack.

One of the primary focuses of DHS is the detection and tracking of nuclear materials. Advanced scanning devices and radiation detection systems are deployed at various entry points, such as airports, seaports, and border crossings, to identify any illicit movement of radioactive materials. These technologies utilize gamma-ray spectrometry, neutron activation analysis, and other techniques to accurately identify and quantify the presence of nuclear materials.

In addition to securing transportation routes, security protocols have been established for nuclear facilities and transportation. Enhanced access controls, rigorous background checks, and continuous monitoring are implemented to prevent unauthorized access and ensure the safety of these facilities. Furthermore, cybersecurity measures are in place to protect against potential terrorist hacking of nuclear systems, including firewalls, encryption, and regular vulnerability assessments.

The radiation detection and monitoring strategies employed by DHS involve the deployment of a network of sensors and detectors across the country. These sensors can quickly identify and locate any abnormal radiation levels, enabling a swift response to potential threats. Additionally, intelligence gathering on terrorist organizations' interest in dirty bombs is a critical aspect of DHS efforts. By closely monitoring and analyzing communications, financial transactions, and other activities, intelligence agencies can identify potential threats and take proactive measures to prevent attacks.

International cooperation and information sharing are pivotal in combating the threat of dirty bombs. DHS collaborates with partner countries, sharing intelligence, best practices, and technological advancements to develop a comprehensive global defense against nuclear terrorism. This collaboration includes joint exercises, capacity-building programs, and the exchange of experts to enhance preparedness and response capabilities.

To ensure effective emergency response and preparedness for dirty bomb incidents, DHS has developed comprehensive plans and protocols. These plans outline the roles and responsibilities of various agencies, establish communication channels, and provide guidance on evacuation, decontamination, and medical treatment.

Public awareness campaigns are also integral to DHS efforts. By educating the public about the dangers of dirty bombs and the importance of vigilance, individuals can become the first line of defense in identifying and reporting suspicious activities. Additionally, legal frameworks and penalties have been established to deter individuals involved in dirty bomb activities.

Finally, research and development initiatives are continuously pursued to advance technologies and enhance prevention efforts. Improved detectors, remote sensing technologies, and data analytics are being explored to detect and track nuclear materials more efficiently and accurately.

In conclusion, the current technologies for detecting nuclear materials are crucial in the fight against dirty bombs. Through the implementation of advanced detection systems, security protocols, cybersecurity measures, intelligence gathering, international cooperation, and public awareness campaigns, DHS is working tirelessly to prevent the making of a dirty bomb by terrorists. However, the ongoing research and development efforts remain paramount in staying ahead of the evolving threat landscape and ensuring the security of our nation.

Advancements in Nuclear Materials Tracking

In recent years, the threat of a dirty bomb attack has become an increasing concern for security agents and the Department of Homeland Security. The potential devastation that a dirty bomb could cause is unimaginable, and as such, efforts to prevent terrorists from obtaining and using nuclear materials have intensified. Advancements in nuclear materials tracking have played a crucial role in these efforts, providing security agents with the tools and technology needed to detect and prevent the illicit trafficking of radioactive materials.

One of the key components of nuclear materials tracking is the development of advanced detection technologies. These technologies utilize various methods, such as radiation detectors and spectroscopy, to identify and analyze radioactive materials. The use of these technologies has significantly improved the ability to detect and track nuclear materials, both at nuclear facilities and in transportation. By implementing these detection systems, security agents can identify suspicious activities and intercept potential threats before they reach their intended targets.

In addition to detection technologies, security protocols for nuclear facilities and transportation have been enhanced to ensure the safe and secure handling of radioactive materials. These protocols include strict access control measures, background checks for personnel, and regular inspections of facilities and vehicles. By implementing these security measures, the risk of unauthorized access to nuclear materials is significantly reduced.

Cybersecurity measures have also been implemented to prevent terrorist hacking of nuclear systems. As technology advances, so does the risk of cyber-attacks. To counter this threat, nuclear facilities have implemented robust cybersecurity systems to protect their networks and prevent unauthorized access. Regular cybersecurity audits and training programs are conducted to ensure the highest level of protection against potential cyber threats.

Intelligence gathering on terrorist organizations' interest in dirty bombs has also been a priority for security agencies. Through international cooperation and information sharing, intelligence agencies are able to track and monitor the activities of terrorist groups and identify any potential threats related to dirty bombs. This information is crucial in preventing terrorist attacks and apprehending those involved in planning or attempting to acquire nuclear materials.

Emergency response plans and preparedness for dirty bomb incidents are also a critical aspect of nuclear materials tracking. By developing comprehensive response plans, security agencies can effectively respond to and mitigate the impact of a dirty bomb attack. These plans include coordination with local law enforcement, evacuation procedures, and medical response protocols. Regular drills and exercises are conducted to test the effectiveness of these plans and identify areas for improvement.

Public awareness campaigns have also been launched to educate the general public about the dangers of dirty bombs. By raising awareness about the potential consequences of a dirty bomb attack, individuals are more likely to report suspicious activities and cooperate with security agencies in their efforts to prevent such attacks.

Legal frameworks and penalties for individuals involved in dirty bomb activities have been strengthened to deter potential terrorists. Harsh penalties and strict enforcement of these laws serve as a strong deterrent and send a clear message that the acquisition and use of nuclear materials for terrorist purposes will not be tolerated.

Finally, research and development of advanced technologies continue to drive advancements in nuclear materials tracking. Scientists and engineers are constantly working on innovative solutions to enhance the prevention efforts of dirty bomb attacks. From improved detection technologies to more secure transportation methods, these advancements are essential in staying one step ahead of potential threats.

In conclusion, advancements in nuclear materials tracking have significantly improved the ability of security agents and the Department of Homeland Security to detect, track, and prevent the illicit trafficking of radioactive materials. From enhanced detection technologies to robust security protocols and international cooperation, these advancements are crucial in the fight against the making of a dirty bomb by terrorists. By staying vigilant, investing in research and development, and fostering international partnerships, security agents are better equipped to protect our nations from the devastating consequences of a dirty bomb attack.

Challenges in Detecting and Tracking Nuclear Materials

The threat of a dirty bomb looms large in today's world, and it is of utmost importance for security agents to understand the challenges associated with detecting and tracking nuclear materials. In this subchapter, we will explore the various hurdles faced by security agencies in their fight against the creation and use of dirty bombs.

One of the primary challenges in this regard is the advancement of nuclear materials detection and tracking technologies. Terrorist organizations are constantly evolving, and so are their methods of obtaining and hiding nuclear materials. Security agents must stay one step ahead by continuously innovating and improving their detection technologies to ensure that no potential threat goes unnoticed.

Another crucial aspect is the establishment of robust security protocols for nuclear facilities and transportation. These protocols must be strictly adhered to and include measures such as stringent background checks, surveillance systems, and secure transportation methods to prevent unauthorized access to nuclear materials.

Cybersecurity measures also play a crucial role in preventing terrorist hacking of nuclear systems. In today's interconnected world, digital vulnerabilities can be exploited by terrorists to gain access to sensitive information or disrupt critical infrastructure. Constant monitoring and upgrading of cybersecurity systems are necessary to counter this threat effectively.

Radiation detection and monitoring strategies are vital in identifying the presence of radioactive materials. However, the challenge lies in differentiating between naturally occurring radioactive sources and those used for nefarious purposes. Security agents must continuously enhance their knowledge and expertise in radiation detection to accurately identify potential threats.

Intelligence gathering on terrorist organizations' interest in dirty bombs is a critical aspect of prevention. Security agencies must collaborate with international partners to collect and share information on the activities and intentions of such organizations. This exchange of intelligence can provide valuable insights and aid in proactive measures to counter the threat.

International cooperation and information sharing on nuclear threats are equally important. The fight against dirty bombs is a global effort, and close collaboration between nations is necessary to combat this menace effectively. Joint exercises, information exchange platforms, and international agreements play a pivotal role in this regard.

Emergency response plans and preparedness for dirty bomb incidents are essential for minimizing the impact in case of an attack. Security agents must work closely with emergency response teams to develop comprehensive plans that encompass evacuation strategies, medical support, and containment measures to mitigate the consequences of a dirty bomb explosion.

Public awareness campaigns on the dangers of dirty bombs can also contribute significantly to prevention efforts. By educating the public about the risks associated with these weapons, individuals can become more vigilant and report suspicious activities, ultimately strengthening the overall security landscape.

Legal frameworks and penalties for individuals involved in dirty bomb activities are necessary to deter potential perpetrators. Strict regulations and severe consequences act as a deterrent and send a clear message that the creation and use of dirty bombs will not be tolerated.

Finally, research and development of advanced technologies are crucial to enhance dirty bomb prevention efforts. Constant innovation can lead to the discovery of new detection methods and materials that can significantly enhance security agents' ability to detect and track nuclear materials.

In conclusion, the challenges in detecting and tracking nuclear materials are multifaceted. However, by addressing these challenges head-on and adopting a proactive approach, security agents can effectively mitigate the threat of dirty bombs and safeguard the well-being of nations and their citizens.

Chapter 3: Security Protocols for Nuclear Facilities and Transportation

Physical Security Measures for Nuclear Facilities

Nuclear facilities are critical infrastructures that require robust physical security measures to prevent unauthorized access, sabotage, theft, and potential use of nuclear materials in the making of dirty bombs. The Department of Homeland Security (DHS) has been actively involved in developing and implementing security protocols to safeguard these facilities and prevent terrorist attacks. This subchapter will explore various physical security measures employed by nuclear facilities, aimed at ensuring the safety of nuclear materials and preventing their misuse by terrorists.

One of the primary physical security measures employed by nuclear facilities is access control. This involves the use of multiple layers of security, such as fences, barriers, and surveillance systems, to deter and detect unauthorized individuals attempting to gain entry. Highly trained security personnel are deployed at entrances and checkpoints to verify the identity and credentials of individuals, ensuring only authorized personnel have access.

In addition to access control, nuclear facilities employ advanced detection technologies to identify and track nuclear materials. These include radiation detection devices and monitoring systems that can quickly identify any unusual levels of radiation, signaling a potential threat. These systems are regularly tested and calibrated to ensure their accuracy and reliability.

To protect against cyber threats, nuclear facilities have implemented robust cybersecurity measures. These measures include firewalls, intrusion detection systems, and strict access controls to prevent unauthorized access to critical systems. Regular vulnerability assessments and penetration testing are conducted to identify and address any potential weaknesses in the cybersecurity infrastructure.

Intelligence gathering plays a crucial role in preventing the making of dirty bombs. Nuclear facilities work closely with intelligence agencies to gather information on terrorist organizations' interest in dirty bombs. This information is used to enhance security protocols and respond proactively to potential threats.

International cooperation and information sharing are vital in combating nuclear threats. Nuclear facilities collaborate with international partners, sharing information on emerging threats, best practices, and technological advancements. This collaboration fosters a global effort to prevent the making of dirty bombs.

Emergency response plans and preparedness are crucial in the event of a dirty bomb incident. Nuclear facilities have well-developed emergency response plans that include evacuation procedures, decontamination protocols, and coordination with local law enforcement and emergency management agencies.

Public awareness campaigns play a vital role in educating the public about the dangers of dirty bombs. Nuclear facilities actively engage with communities, conducting outreach programs, and disseminating information through various channels to raise awareness and promote vigilance.

Legal frameworks and penalties for individuals involved in dirty bomb activities act as a deterrent. Strict laws and severe penalties serve as a warning to potential perpetrators, ensuring that those involved in the making of dirty bombs face significant consequences.

Lastly, continuous research and development of advanced technologies are critical in enhancing dirty bomb prevention efforts. Nuclear facilities invest in cutting-edge technologies to improve detection capabilities, enhance physical security measures, and stay one step ahead of potential threats.

In conclusion, physical security measures employed by nuclear facilities are essential to prevent the making of dirty bombs. Through access control, detection technologies, cybersecurity measures, intelligence gathering, international cooperation, emergency preparedness, public awareness campaigns, legal frameworks, and research and development, nuclear facilities work tirelessly to protect nuclear materials and ensure the safety and security of our communities.

Transportation Security Protocols for Nuclear Materials

Transporting nuclear materials poses a significant threat to national security, as terrorists can exploit vulnerabilities in the transportation process to obtain these materials for the creation of dirty bombs. To counter this threat, robust transportation security protocols must be implemented to ensure the safe and secure transport of nuclear materials.

One of the key elements in transportation security protocols is the use of advanced detection and tracking technologies. These technologies enable security agents to identify and monitor the movement of nuclear materials, ensuring that they are not diverted or tampered with during transit. State-of-the-art radiation detection equipment plays a crucial role in this process, as it can identify the presence of radioactive materials and enable swift response measures.

In addition to detection technologies, cybersecurity measures are also vital to prevent terrorist hacking of nuclear systems. The Department of Homeland Security works tirelessly to develop and implement robust cybersecurity protocols to safeguard nuclear transportation systems from cyber threats. This includes the use of encryption, firewalls, and multi-factor authentication to protect against unauthorized access and potential sabotage.

Furthermore, intelligence gathering on terrorist organizations' interest in dirty bombs is paramount. Through close collaboration with intelligence agencies, security agents can stay one step ahead by identifying potential threats and taking proactive measures to prevent them. This includes monitoring online communications, tracking suspicious activities, and infiltrating terrorist networks to gather crucial information.

International cooperation and information sharing play a crucial role in addressing the threat of dirty bombs. By collaborating with other countries and sharing intelligence, security agents can enhance their understanding of global nuclear threats and develop effective countermeasures. This partnership also facilitates the exchange of best practices, technology sharing, and joint training exercises to improve transportation security protocols worldwide.

Emergency response plans and preparedness are essential components of transportation security protocols. Security agents must develop comprehensive plans to respond swiftly and effectively in the event of a dirty bomb incident. This includes establishing evacuation procedures, setting up decontamination sites, and coordinating with local law enforcement and emergency response teams.

Public awareness campaigns are crucial to educate the public about the dangers of dirty bombs and to encourage vigilance. By raising awareness, individuals can play a vital role in identifying and reporting suspicious activities, thus acting as an additional layer of defense against potential threats.

To deter individuals involved in dirty bomb activities, legal frameworks and penalties must be established. Strict laws should be enacted to punish those who engage in the creation, possession, or transport of dirty bombs. These penalties serve as a deterrent and send a strong message that such activities will not be tolerated.

Research and development of advanced technologies are ongoing in order to enhance dirty bomb prevention efforts. Continuous innovation is necessary to stay ahead of evolving threats and to develop more effective detection, tracking, and response systems. By investing in research and development, security agents can strengthen their capabilities and enhance the safety and security of nuclear material transportation.

In conclusion, transportation security protocols for nuclear materials are essential to safeguard against the threat of dirty bombs. By employing advanced detection and tracking technologies, implementing cybersecurity measures, gathering intelligence, fostering international cooperation, developing emergency response plans, raising public awareness, establishing legal frameworks, and investing in research and development, security agents can significantly enhance their ability to prevent the creation and transport of dirty bombs, thus ensuring the safety and security of nations around the world.

Ensuring Safety during Nuclear Material Transfers

The transfer of nuclear materials poses a significant risk if not handled with utmost care and security. In this subchapter, we will delve into the various measures and protocols that need to be in place to ensure the safety of nuclear material transfers. By understanding these procedures, security agents can effectively mitigate the risk of terrorists obtaining these materials and using them to create a dirty bomb.

One crucial aspect of ensuring safety during nuclear material transfers is the use of advanced detection and tracking technologies. By implementing state-of-the-art equipment, security agents can identify any attempts to tamper with or steal nuclear materials. These technologies, such as radiation detectors and tracking devices, enable real-time monitoring of the materials throughout the transfer process.

In addition to technological measures, security protocols play a vital role in safeguarding nuclear facilities and transportation. Strict access control, background checks, and comprehensive training for personnel involved in the transfer process are essential. By strictly adhering to these protocols, security agents can minimize the risk of insider threats and unauthorized access to nuclear materials.

In the digital age, cybersecurity measures are crucial to prevent terrorist hacking of nuclear systems. By implementing robust cybersecurity protocols, such as regular system updates, encryption, and intrusion detection systems, security agents can thwart any attempts to compromise the security of nuclear facilities and transportation networks.

Radiation detection and monitoring strategies are also key components of ensuring safety during nuclear material transfers. By deploying radiation detection devices at various checkpoints, security agents can identify any unauthorized presence of nuclear materials and respond promptly to potential threats.

Intelligence gathering on terrorist organizations' interest in dirty bombs is another critical aspect of preventing their creation. By actively monitoring and analyzing intelligence, security agents can identify potential threats and take appropriate preventive measures to counter them.

International cooperation and information sharing on nuclear threats are essential for comprehensive security. By collaborating with other countries, sharing intelligence, and collectively addressing nuclear threats, security agents can enhance their capabilities to prevent the making of dirty bombs.

Emergency response plans and preparedness for dirty bomb incidents are vital to minimize the consequences of an attack. By having well-coordinated response plans, including evacuation procedures, decontamination protocols, and medical assistance, security agents can effectively manage the aftermath of a dirty bomb incident.

Public awareness campaigns play a crucial role in educating the public about the dangers of dirty bombs. By disseminating information about the potential consequences of such attacks, security agents can enlist public support in preventing the creation and use of dirty bombs.

Legal frameworks and penalties for individuals involved in dirty bomb activities serve as deterrents. By enacting strict laws and imposing severe penalties, security agents can discourage individuals from engaging in any activities related to dirty bombs.

Finally, ongoing research and development of advanced technologies are essential to enhance dirty bomb prevention efforts. By investing in innovative solutions, security agents can stay ahead of emerging threats and continuously improve their ability to detect and prevent the making of dirty bombs.

In conclusion, ensuring safety during nuclear material transfers requires a multi-faceted approach that encompasses advanced technologies, security protocols, cybersecurity measures, intelligence gathering, international cooperation, emergency response plans, public awareness campaigns, legal frameworks, and continuous research and development. By diligently implementing these measures, security agents can effectively combat the threat of dirty bombs and protect national security.

Chapter 4: Cybersecurity Measures to Prevent Terrorist Hacking of Nuclear Systems

Vulnerabilities of Nuclear Systems to Cyberattacks

In today's interconnected world, the threat of cyberattacks has become increasingly prevalent, extending its reach to critical infrastructures such as nuclear systems. This subchapter aims to shed light on the vulnerabilities of nuclear systems to cyberattacks and the urgent need for robust cybersecurity measures to prevent potential terrorist hacking.

Nuclear facilities and transportation networks are prime targets for cybercriminals due to the catastrophic consequences that could result from a successful attack. The potential of a dirty bomb, a conventional explosive device combined with radioactive materials, falling into the hands of terrorists poses a grave threat to national security. The Department of Homeland Security (DHS) has been working tirelessly to counter these threats and safeguard the nation against the making of a dirty bomb.

One of the key vulnerabilities of nuclear systems lies in their increasing reliance on digital systems and networks. As these systems become more interconnected, they become more susceptible to cyberattacks. A successful attack on a nuclear facility's control systems could have devastating consequences, leading to the theft of radioactive materials or even a catastrophic release of radiation.

To address these vulnerabilities, stringent security protocols are required for both nuclear facilities and transportation networks. Regular security audits and risk assessments are crucial in identifying potential weaknesses and implementing necessary security measures. This includes physical security enhancements, access controls, and surveillance systems to deter and detect unauthorized access.

Furthermore, cybersecurity measures must be implemented to prevent terrorist hacking of nuclear systems. These measures involve robust firewalls, intrusion detection systems, and encryption protocols to secure critical networks and prevent unauthorized access. Regular cybersecurity training for personnel is also essential to ensure awareness of the evolving cyber threat landscape and the adoption of best practices.

Effective radiation detection and monitoring strategies are also vital in mitigating the risk of a dirty bomb incident. The deployment of advanced detection technologies, such as radiation sensors and monitoring systems, can help identify potential threats and provide early warning to security agents. Additionally, intelligence gathering on terrorist organizations' interest in dirty bombs is crucial for proactive prevention.

International cooperation and information sharing play a pivotal role in combating nuclear threats. Close collaboration between countries, intelligence agencies, and law enforcement bodies is essential to exchange information on emerging threats and share best practices. This collective effort enhances the overall security posture and minimizes the chances of successful attacks.

Emergency response plans and preparedness for dirty bomb incidents are equally important. Regular drills and simulations enable security agents to effectively respond to such incidents, minimizing the potential damage and ensuring public safety. Public awareness campaigns are also necessary to educate and inform the general public about the dangers of dirty bombs, encouraging vigilance and reporting any suspicious activities.

To deter individuals involved in dirty bomb activities, robust legal frameworks and penalties must be established. Strict enforcement of laws and severe consequences for those engaged in illicit activities related to dirty bombs serve as a strong deterrent.

Finally, ongoing research and development of advanced technologies are vital to enhance dirty bomb prevention efforts. Investment in cutting-edge technologies, such as artificial intelligence, machine learning, and quantum encryption, can help stay ahead of cyber threats and strengthen the overall resilience of nuclear systems.

In conclusion, the vulnerabilities of nuclear systems to cyberattacks pose a significant threat to national security. The comprehensive implementation of security protocols, cybersecurity measures, radiation detection strategies, intelligence gathering, international cooperation, emergency response plans, public awareness campaigns, legal frameworks, and technological advancements are essential in preventing the making of a dirty bomb. By addressing these vulnerabilities head-on, security agents and the Department of Homeland Security can effectively combat this grave threat and ensure the safety of the nation.

Safeguarding Nuclear Facilities from Cyber Threats

In recent years, the world has witnessed an alarming increase in cyber threats targeting critical infrastructure, including nuclear facilities. The potential consequences of a successful cyber attack on a nuclear facility are devastating, making it essential for security agents to understand and implement effective cybersecurity measures. This subchapter aims to provide crucial insights into safeguarding nuclear facilities from cyber threats, ensuring the safety and security of these vital installations.

The threat of cyber attacks on nuclear facilities has become more sophisticated and prevalent. Terrorist organizations and malicious actors are constantly seeking ways to exploit vulnerabilities in the digital systems that control and monitor nuclear facilities. The consequences of a successful cyber attack on these systems could range from unauthorized access to critical information, tampering with safety protocols, or even the manipulation of nuclear processes, leading to catastrophic outcomes.

To counter these threats, security agents must be well-versed in the latest cybersecurity measures. This includes implementing robust firewalls, intrusion detection systems, and encryption protocols to protect against unauthorized access. Regular vulnerability assessments and penetration testing should be conducted to identify and address any weaknesses in the system.

Furthermore, close coordination and information sharing among national and international agencies are crucial in preventing cyber attacks on nuclear facilities. Intelligence gathering on terrorist organizations' interest in dirty bombs and sharing this information across borders can help identify potential threats before they materialize. International cooperation also plays a significant role in the exchange of best practices and technological advancements to enhance cybersecurity efforts.

In addition to cyber threats, security agents must also focus on radiation detection and monitoring strategies within nuclear facilities. Advanced technologies, such as remote sensing and real-time monitoring systems, can enhance the detection of radiation leaks or unauthorized movement of nuclear materials.

Emergency response plans and preparedness for dirty bomb incidents should be in place to ensure a swift and effective response in case of an attack. Regular drills and training exercises should be conducted to familiarize security agents with the necessary protocols and procedures.

Public awareness campaigns are crucial to educating the general population about the dangers of dirty bombs. By raising public awareness, individuals can become the eyes and ears of law enforcement agencies, reporting any suspicious activities or potential threats.

Lastly, legal frameworks and penalties for individuals involved in dirty bomb activities should be robust and comprehensive. The legal consequences must act as a strong deterrent against engaging in such activities.

In conclusion, safeguarding nuclear facilities from cyber threats requires a multi-faceted approach, with a focus on advanced cybersecurity measures, radiation detection technologies, international cooperation, emergency response plans, public awareness campaigns, and stringent legal frameworks. By implementing these measures, security agents can ensure the safety and security of nuclear facilities, preventing terrorists from acquiring the materials necessary for the making of a dirty bomb.

Collaboration between Cybersecurity Experts and Nuclear Industry

In today's interconnected world, the collaboration between cybersecurity experts and the nuclear industry has become paramount in ensuring the safety and security of our nations. This subchapter delves into the critical partnership between these two entities, highlighting their joint efforts in combating the threat of dirty bombs and safeguarding our homeland.

The Department of Homeland Security, in its relentless pursuit of thwarting terrorist activities, has recognized the need for a strong alliance between cybersecurity experts and the nuclear industry. Cybersecurity measures are now an integral part of nuclear facilities' security protocols, as they are instrumental in preventing terrorist hacking of nuclear systems. With the potential catastrophic consequences of such attacks, it is imperative that the nuclear industry remains at the forefront of cybersecurity advancements.

Nuclear materials detection and tracking technologies have also seen significant developments through collaboration between cybersecurity experts and the nuclear industry. These technologies play a vital role in identifying and monitoring the movement of nuclear materials, making it harder for terrorists to acquire them for the manufacturing of dirty bombs. By leveraging cyber capabilities, experts have enhanced the efficiency and accuracy of these detection systems, minimizing the risk posed by illicit nuclear material transfers.

Intelligence gathering on terrorist organizations' interest in dirty bombs is another area where collaboration has proved invaluable. Through information sharing and international cooperation, cybersecurity experts and the nuclear industry have bolstered their ability to identify and assess potential threats. By staying one step ahead of these terrorist organizations, security agents can better implement preventive measures and neutralize potential threats before they materialize.

Emergency response plans and preparedness for dirty bomb incidents have also benefited greatly from the collaboration between cybersecurity experts and the nuclear industry. By leveraging cyber technologies, experts have developed sophisticated monitoring and radiation detection strategies, ensuring a prompt and effective response in the event of a dirty bomb incident. This collaborative effort has significantly enhanced our emergency response capabilities, minimizing the potential impact of such attacks.

Furthermore, public awareness campaigns on the dangers of dirty bombs have been successful in large part due to the collaboration between these two entities. By combining their expertise, cybersecurity experts and the nuclear industry have effectively conveyed the severity of the threat, ensuring that the public remains informed and vigilant.

In conclusion, the collaboration between cybersecurity experts and the nuclear industry is an essential component in the fight against dirty bombs. Through their combined efforts, security agents can better navigate the challenges posed by terrorism, ensuring the safety and security of our nations. This subchapter highlights the importance of this partnership and serves as a guide for those involved in the making of a dirty bomb and the Department of Homeland Security's efforts to prevent it.

Chapter 5: Radiation Detection and Monitoring Strategies

Technologies for Detecting Radiation

Radiation detection and monitoring strategies play a crucial role in preventing the creation and detonation of dirty bombs. These technologies are essential in safeguarding our nation against the threat of nuclear terrorism. In this subchapter, we will explore the various technologies employed by security agents to detect radiation and protect our homeland.

One of the primary technologies used for detecting radiation is the radiation detection portal monitor. These monitors are installed at key checkpoints such as airports, seaports, and border crossings. They use sophisticated sensors to scan individuals, vehicles, and cargo for the presence of radioactive materials. The portal monitors provide real-time results, enabling security agents to identify and isolate potential threats quickly.

Another critical technology in radiation detection is the handheld radiation detector. These portable devices allow security agents to scan suspicious items or areas for the presence of radioactive materials. Handheld detectors are especially useful in situations where immediate response is required, such as during security sweeps or emergency incidents.

In recent years, advancements in technology have led to the development of more sophisticated radiation detection systems. These include the use of gamma-ray spectrometry, which enables security agents to identify the specific type of radioactive material present. This information is crucial in determining the potential threat level and in devising an appropriate response strategy.

Furthermore, the use of unmanned aerial vehicles (UAVs) equipped with radiation detection sensors has revolutionized radiation monitoring. These UAVs can cover large areas quickly, providing real-time data on radiation levels and hotspots. This technology allows security agents to identify and respond to potential threats more effectively.

To enhance radiation detection capabilities, the Department of Homeland Security has also invested in research and development of advanced technologies. This includes the exploration of artificial intelligence and machine learning algorithms to improve the accuracy and speed of radiation detection systems.

In conclusion, the development and utilization of technologies for detecting radiation play a critical role in our efforts to prevent the creation and detonation of dirty bombs. These technologies, including radiation detection portal monitors, handheld detectors, gamma-ray spectrometry, UAVs, and advanced algorithms, enable security agents to identify and respond to potential threats swiftly and effectively. By staying at the forefront of technological advancements, we can enhance our dirty bomb prevention efforts and ensure the safety and security of our nation.

Monitoring Systems for Radiation Levels

In the fight against the making of a dirty bomb, monitoring systems for radiation levels play a crucial role in safeguarding national security. These systems are designed to detect and track nuclear materials, ensuring their secure transportation and preventing their unauthorized use by terrorists. This subchapter explores the various monitoring technologies and strategies employed by the Department of Homeland Security (DHS) and security agents in their efforts to combat this grave threat.

One of the key components of radiation monitoring systems is the use of advanced detection and tracking technologies. These include gamma-ray spectrometry, neutron detectors, and gamma-ray imaging systems. These state-of-the-art technologies enable security agents to identify and locate potential sources of radiation accurately. Additionally, the DHS has invested in the development of portable radiation detectors, allowing agents to conduct on-site inspections of suspicious objects or individuals.

To enhance the security of nuclear facilities and transportation, stringent security protocols have been put in place. These protocols involve the use of access controls, radiation portal monitors, and vehicle screening systems. By implementing these measures, security agents can detect and deter any illicit attempt to access or transport nuclear materials.

In an increasingly digital world, cybersecurity measures are essential to prevent terrorist hacking of nuclear systems. The DHS has established robust cybersecurity protocols to safeguard critical infrastructure from cyber threats. These measures include network security, encryption, and continuous monitoring of digital systems to detect any suspicious activities.

Intelligence gathering plays a pivotal role in understanding terrorist organizations' interest in dirty bombs. By gathering and analyzing intelligence from various sources, security agents can identify potential threats and take proactive measures to prevent their realization. International cooperation and information sharing are crucial in this regard, as they enable the exchange of intelligence and best practices between nations.

In the event of a dirty bomb incident, emergency response plans and preparedness are vital. These plans involve coordination between law enforcement agencies, first responders, and public health authorities. Regular drills and exercises are conducted to ensure a seamless response to such incidents, minimizing casualties and containing the spread of radiation.

Public awareness campaigns play a significant role in educating the public about the dangers of dirty bombs. By raising awareness about the potential consequences, individuals are more likely to report suspicious activities and become active partners in national security efforts.

Legal frameworks and penalties are essential to deter individuals involved in dirty bomb activities. Strict laws and severe penalties act as a deterrent, ensuring that those who engage in such activities face the full force of the law.

Finally, ongoing research and development of advanced technologies further enhance dirty bomb prevention efforts. The DHS continually invests in innovative solutions, such as the development of new detection systems and enhanced data analytics, to stay ahead of evolving threats.

In conclusion, monitoring systems for radiation levels form a critical component of the DHS's comprehensive efforts to combat the making of a dirty bomb. By employing advanced technologies, implementing stringent security protocols, and fostering international cooperation, security agents are at the forefront of safeguarding national security and preventing this grave threat.

Importance of Continuous Monitoring in High-Risk Areas

High-risk areas, such as nuclear facilities or transportation routes for nuclear materials, pose a significant threat to national security. The potential for terrorists to acquire and use these materials in the creation of a dirty bomb is a persistent concern for security agents and the Department of Homeland Security. In order to effectively combat this threat, continuous monitoring of these areas is of utmost importance.

Continuous monitoring provides real-time information on the status and integrity of high-risk areas. It allows security agents to detect any unauthorized access, potential breaches, or suspicious activities that could indicate an impending threat. By constantly monitoring these areas, security agents can quickly respond to any security breaches, preventing terrorists from gaining access to sensitive materials and reducing the risk of a dirty bomb incident.

One key aspect of continuous monitoring is the use of advanced nuclear materials detection and tracking technologies. These technologies help security agents identify any anomalies or irregularities in the movement and storage of nuclear materials. By tracking the movement of these materials, security agents can closely monitor their whereabouts and detect any attempts to divert or steal them.

In addition to nuclear materials detection and tracking technologies, security protocols play a crucial role in ensuring the safety of high-risk areas. These protocols outline the procedures for access control, personnel screening, and security measures to be implemented. Continuous monitoring allows security agents to ensure that these protocols are being followed and to address any deviations or vulnerabilities promptly.

The importance of continuous monitoring extends beyond physical security measures. Cybersecurity measures are equally vital in preventing terrorist hacking of nuclear systems. Continuous monitoring of cyber systems can help identify and mitigate any cybersecurity threats, ensuring that critical infrastructure remains secure from potential attacks.

Radiation detection and monitoring strategies are also essential in high-risk areas. Continuous monitoring of radiation levels helps security agents identify any abnormal radiation signatures that could be indicative of a dirty bomb or illicit nuclear activity. By continuously monitoring radiation levels, security agents can quickly respond to any potential threats and prevent the situation from escalating.

Intelligence gathering on terrorist organizations' interest in dirty bombs is another critical aspect of continuous monitoring. By staying updated on the activities and intentions of these organizations, security agents can anticipate potential threats and take proactive measures to prevent the acquisition or use of nuclear materials for malicious purposes.

International cooperation and information sharing play a vital role in continuous monitoring efforts. Collaboration between different countries allows for the exchange of intelligence, best practices, and technological advancements. By sharing information on nuclear threats, countries can collectively work towards enhancing their monitoring capabilities and preventing the proliferation of dirty bombs.

Emergency response plans and preparedness for dirty bomb incidents are essential components of continuous monitoring efforts. By continuously reviewing and updating these plans, security agents can ensure that they are well-prepared to handle any dirty bomb incidents effectively. Regular drills and simulations help identify any gaps in preparedness and provide valuable insights for improvement.

Public awareness campaigns are also crucial in promoting the importance of continuous monitoring and the dangers of dirty bombs. By educating the public about the risks associated with dirty bombs, individuals can become more vigilant and report any suspicious activities, contributing to the overall security efforts.

Legal frameworks and penalties for individuals involved in dirty bomb activities serve as deterrents and provide a legal basis for prosecuting those involved in illicit nuclear activities. Continuous monitoring helps gather evidence and identify individuals who may be engaged in activities related to dirty bombs, ensuring that they are held accountable for their actions.

Finally, research and development of advanced technologies are essential to enhance dirty bomb prevention efforts. Continuous monitoring allows for the testing and implementation of these advanced technologies, ensuring that security agents have access to the latest tools and techniques to combat the evolving threats.

In conclusion, continuous monitoring is of utmost importance in high-risk areas to prevent the making of a dirty bomb by terrorists. By utilizing advanced technologies, implementing strict security protocols, monitoring cyber systems, detecting radiation levels, gathering intelligence, promoting international cooperation, and ensuring emergency preparedness, security agents can effectively mitigate the risks associated with dirty bombs. Through public awareness campaigns, legal frameworks, and continuous research and development, we can enhance our prevention efforts and safeguard national security against this grave threat.

Chapter 6: Intelligence Gathering on Terrorist Organizations' Interest in Dirty Bombs

Role of Intelligence Agencies in Identifying Threats

The Role of Intelligence Agencies in Identifying Threats

In the fight against the making of a dirty bomb and to ensure the safety of our homeland, the role of intelligence agencies is paramount. These agencies play a crucial role in identifying threats and gathering vital information to prevent any potential attacks. This subchapter explores the various ways intelligence agencies contribute to this effort.

One of the key responsibilities of intelligence agencies is gathering intelligence on terrorist organizations' interest in dirty bombs. Through extensive surveillance, infiltrating terrorist networks, and monitoring online activities, these agencies are able to identify potential threats and their intentions. By staying ahead of the game, they can provide valuable information to other security agents and help prevent any attempts at building a dirty bomb.

International cooperation and information sharing are also critical in combating the threat of dirty bombs. Intelligence agencies work closely with their counterparts in other countries to share intelligence and exchange information on nuclear threats. This collaboration allows for a more comprehensive understanding of the global threat landscape and enhances our ability to prevent any potential attacks.

Intelligence agencies also contribute to the development of advanced technologies and research aimed at enhancing dirty bomb prevention efforts. By investing in research and development, these agencies ensure that we stay ahead of the ever-evolving threat landscape. From nuclear materials detection and tracking technologies to cybersecurity measures and radiation detection strategies, intelligence agencies play a crucial role in driving innovation in these areas.

Additionally, intelligence agencies are instrumental in the formulation of emergency response plans and preparedness for dirty bomb incidents. By analyzing potential scenarios and collecting intelligence on potential targets, they help shape effective emergency response strategies. This ensures that in the event of an attack, the response is swift and effective, minimizing the potential damage and loss of life.

Public awareness campaigns on the dangers of dirty bombs are another area where intelligence agencies contribute significantly. By disseminating information to the public, they raise awareness about the threat and empower individuals to be vigilant. This collective effort is essential in preventing attacks and ensuring the safety of our communities.

Lastly, intelligence agencies play a vital role in establishing legal frameworks and penalties for individuals involved in dirty bomb activities. By working closely with lawmakers, they help shape legislation that holds individuals accountable for their actions. This acts as a deterrent and strengthens our ability to prosecute those involved in the making of a dirty bomb.

In conclusion, intelligence agencies are at the forefront of identifying threats and preventing the making of a dirty bomb. Through their intelligence gathering, international cooperation, research and development, emergency preparedness efforts, public awareness campaigns, and legal frameworks, they play a crucial role in safeguarding our nation. Their efforts are essential in the ongoing fight against terrorism and ensuring the safety and security of our homeland.

Methods of Collecting Information on Terrorist Activities

In the ongoing battle against terrorism, it is imperative for security agents to stay one step ahead of the ever-evolving tactics used by these dangerous groups. Collecting accurate and timely information on terrorist activities is crucial to prevent catastrophic incidents, such as the making of a dirty bomb. This subchapter explores various methods that can be employed to gather valuable intelligence on terrorist organizations' interest in dirty bombs, ensuring the safety and security of the nation.

One of the key methods is intelligence gathering through human sources. Security agents rely on informants, undercover agents, and confidential sources who infiltrate terrorist organizations and provide valuable insights into their activities. These individuals play a critical role in identifying potential threats and gathering information on their plans to acquire or construct a dirty bomb.

Additionally, technological advancements have significantly enhanced the collection of information on terrorist activities. Surveillance systems, satellite imagery, and drones equipped with advanced sensors can be utilized to monitor suspicious activities and locations. These technologies aid in tracking the movement of individuals, identifying potential nuclear materials smuggling routes, and detecting any illicit activities related to dirty bomb production.

Furthermore, cybersecurity measures are essential to prevent terrorist hacking of nuclear systems. As terrorists become more technologically sophisticated, it is crucial to protect nuclear facilities' computer networks from cyber-attacks. Robust cybersecurity protocols, such as firewalls, encryption, and frequent system updates, ensure the integrity and confidentiality of sensitive information.

International cooperation and information sharing play a vital role in combating nuclear threats. Security agents must collaborate with intelligence agencies and law enforcement organizations worldwide to exchange information on potential terrorist activities. These partnerships facilitate the identification of global networks involved in the production and trafficking of nuclear materials.

Emergency response plans and preparedness are equally important aspects of preventing dirty bomb incidents. Security agents must develop comprehensive strategies to effectively respond to and mitigate the consequences of a dirty bomb attack. Regular drills and simulations help refine these plans, ensuring a coordinated and swift response in the event of an incident.

Public awareness campaigns are also crucial in educating the general public about the dangers of dirty bombs. By raising awareness and promoting a culture of vigilance, citizens become active participants in preventing terrorist activities and reporting suspicious behaviors.

Finally, legal frameworks and penalties for individuals involved in dirty bomb activities serve as strong deterrents. Strict laws and severe punishments act as a deterrent to potential terrorists, making it significantly harder for them to carry out their malicious plans.

To stay ahead of terrorists, continuous research and development of advanced technologies is imperative. These efforts aim to enhance dirty bomb prevention, detection, and mitigation strategies. By investing in cutting-edge technologies, security agents can adapt to the ever-changing threat landscape and effectively safeguard the nation against potential dirty bomb attacks.

In conclusion, the methods of collecting information on terrorist activities are diverse and multifaceted. From human intelligence sources to advanced surveillance systems, each method plays a critical role in preventing the making of a dirty bomb. The combination of these strategies, along with international cooperation, public awareness campaigns, and stringent legal frameworks, ensures the effective protection of nuclear facilities and the safety of the nation.

Analyzing and Assessing Terrorist Intentions and Capabilities

In the subchapter "Analyzing and Assessing Terrorist Intentions and Capabilities" of the book "Inside the Threat: The Making of a Dirty Bomb and Homeland Security's Fight to Stop It," we delve into the crucial task of understanding the motivations and capabilities of terrorists who seek to create a dirty bomb. This subchapter is specifically tailored to the knowledge needs of security agents who play a vital role in safeguarding our nation against this grave threat.

To effectively combat the making of a dirty bomb, security agents must possess a deep understanding of the entire process, from the acquisition of nuclear materials to the assembly and deployment of the bomb. This subchapter provides an in-depth examination of various aspects related to this threat, including nuclear materials detection and tracking technologies, security protocols for nuclear facilities and transportation, and cybersecurity measures to prevent terrorist hacking of nuclear systems.

Furthermore, intelligence gathering on terrorist organizations' interest in dirty bombs is crucial for identifying potential threats before they materialize. This subchapter explores the methodologies and strategies employed by security agencies to gather actionable intelligence on terrorist intentions and capabilities, enabling proactive measures to disrupt their plans.

International cooperation and information sharing play a vital role in combating the threat of dirty bombs. This subchapter emphasizes the importance of collaboration between nations, sharing intelligence, best practices, and technological advancements to enhance our collective ability to prevent and respond to nuclear threats.

Emergency response plans and preparedness for dirty bomb incidents are crucial components of a comprehensive security strategy. This subchapter provides insights into the development of effective emergency response plans, training protocols, and coordination mechanisms, ensuring a rapid and efficient response in the event of a dirty bomb incident.

To bolster our defense against dirty bombs, public awareness campaigns are essential. This subchapter explores the significance of educating the public about the dangers associated with dirty bombs, fostering a sense of collective responsibility and vigilance among citizens.

Lastly, legal frameworks and penalties play a pivotal role in deterring individuals involved in dirty bomb activities. This subchapter delves into the existing legal frameworks, highlighting the importance of strict penalties for those engaged in the creation, possession, or use of dirty bombs.

As the threat of dirty bombs continues to evolve, research and development of advanced technologies become paramount. This subchapter highlights ongoing efforts to develop innovative and cutting-edge technologies that enhance our ability to prevent, detect, and respond to the making of dirty bombs.

By delving into these crucial topics, this subchapter equips security agents with the necessary knowledge to effectively analyze and assess terrorist intentions and capabilities regarding the creation of dirty bombs. With this enhanced understanding, security agents can play a pivotal role in safeguarding our nation and countering this significant threat to our security and well-being.

Chapter 7: International Cooperation and Information Sharing on Nuclear Threats

Collaborative Efforts between Countries on Nuclear Security

In the fight against the threat of dirty bombs, collaboration between countries plays a vital role in safeguarding global security. The international community recognizes the urgency and seriousness of this threat, and concerted efforts are being made to prevent terrorists from acquiring and using nuclear materials. This subchapter explores the collaborative initiatives between countries on nuclear security and highlights the various strategies employed to counter this threat.

One of the most critical aspects of collaborative efforts is the sharing of information and intelligence on nuclear threats. Countries are actively engaged in gathering and analyzing intelligence on terrorist organizations' interest in dirty bombs. Through international cooperation, security agents from different nations exchange valuable information, enabling a comprehensive understanding of the evolving threat landscape. This collective intelligence helps in identifying potential targets, tracking suspicious activities, and apprehending individuals involved in dirty bomb activities.

Additionally, countries are working together to enhance the detection and tracking of nuclear materials. Advanced technologies, such as nuclear materials detection and tracking technologies, are being developed through collaborative research and development programs. These technologies enable security agents to identify and locate nuclear materials, both within and outside of nuclear facilities. Furthermore, international cooperation ensures the implementation of robust security protocols for the transportation of nuclear materials, reducing the risk of theft or diversion.

Cybersecurity measures are also a crucial component of collaborative efforts. Countries are sharing best practices and intelligence on preventing terrorist hacking of nuclear systems. By collectively strengthening their cybersecurity infrastructure, nations can minimize the vulnerability of nuclear facilities to cyber-attacks, ensuring that critical systems remain protected.

In addition to prevention, countries are actively engaged in developing emergency response plans and preparedness for dirty bomb incidents. Collaborative efforts enable the sharing of expertise and best practices in handling and mitigating the consequences of a dirty bomb detonation. Through joint training exercises and simulations, security agents gain valuable experience in responding to such incidents, thereby enhancing the overall preparedness and resilience of nations.

Public awareness campaigns also form an integral part of collaborative efforts. By disseminating information on the dangers of dirty bombs to the general public, countries aim to raise awareness and promote vigilance. This collective effort helps in creating a sense of shared responsibility, empowering citizens to report suspicious activities and contribute to overall security.

Lastly, collaborative efforts extend to the development of legal frameworks and penalties for individuals involved in dirty bomb activities. Countries are working together to establish stringent laws and regulations to deter and punish those engaged in the production or use of dirty bombs. By aligning their legal systems, nations can effectively prosecute offenders and dismantle terrorist networks involved in the dirty bomb trade.

In conclusion, collaborative efforts between countries on nuclear security are crucial in preventing the making and usage of dirty bombs by terrorists. Through international cooperation, countries are strengthening their intelligence gathering, enhancing detection technologies, fortifying cybersecurity measures, developing emergency response plans, raising public awareness, and enforcing legal frameworks. By working together, security agents from different nations can effectively combat the threat of dirty bombs and safeguard global security.

Sharing Intelligence and Best Practices

In the fight against the making of a dirty bomb, intelligence gathering and sharing best practices are critical components of Homeland Security's efforts. This subchapter delves into the importance of collaboration, information sharing, and the exchange of best practices among security agents to prevent the creation of a dirty bomb.

The Department of Homeland Security recognizes the gravity of the threat posed by terrorists seeking to obtain and use nuclear materials for malicious purposes. To counter this threat effectively, it is essential for security agents to share intelligence on the tactics, techniques, and procedures employed by these dangerous individuals or organizations.

Sharing intelligence allows security agents to stay one step ahead of potential threats and adapt their strategies accordingly. This includes sharing information on terrorist organizations' interest in dirty bombs, their recruitment methods, and their supply chain networks. By pooling resources and sharing information, security agencies can identify patterns, track potential suspects, and disrupt their operations before they can carry out any attacks.

Furthermore, sharing best practices among security agents is crucial for enhancing security protocols at nuclear facilities and during transportation. It involves the exchange of knowledge on the latest nuclear materials detection and tracking technologies, cybersecurity measures to prevent terrorist hacking of nuclear systems, and radiation detection and monitoring strategies. This collaboration ensures that security measures remain up-to-date and incorporate the latest advancements in technology.

International cooperation is also emphasized in this subchapter. Given the global nature of the threat, it is imperative for security agents worldwide to work together, sharing information and coordinating efforts to combat the making of dirty bombs. This includes establishing channels for information sharing, conducting joint training exercises, and fostering partnerships between countries to enhance overall security.

Emergency response plans and preparedness for dirty bomb incidents are also discussed in this subchapter. Security agents need to be well-prepared to respond swiftly and effectively in the event of a dirty bomb incident. Sharing best practices in emergency response planning and conducting realistic drills can ensure a coordinated and efficient response, minimizing the impact of such an attack.

Public awareness campaigns play a vital role in preventing the making of dirty bombs. Security agents must educate the public about the dangers posed by these weapons and the importance of reporting suspicious activities. This subchapter explores various approaches to raise public awareness and foster a sense of responsibility and vigilance within communities.

Finally, this subchapter addresses the legal frameworks and penalties for individuals involved in dirty bomb activities. By understanding the legal consequences and working within the established frameworks, security agents can ensure that those responsible for planning and executing dirty bomb attacks are held accountable for their actions.

To stay ahead of evolving threats, research and development of advanced technologies are critical. This subchapter explores ongoing efforts to develop innovative technologies that can enhance dirty bomb prevention efforts, such as improved detection systems, advanced surveillance tools, and cutting-edge radiation monitoring devices.

In conclusion, sharing intelligence and best practices is essential in the fight against the making of a dirty bomb. By collaborating, exchanging information, and implementing the most effective strategies, security agents can enhance their capabilities and prevent terrorists from obtaining and using nuclear materials for destructive purposes. This subchapter provides valuable insights and guidance for security agents striving to protect their nations and secure a safer future.

Challenges and Benefits of International Cooperation

In the face of the ever-evolving threat landscape, international cooperation has become increasingly crucial in combating the proliferation of dirty bombs and safeguarding national security. This subchapter explores the challenges and benefits associated with international cooperation in the fight against nuclear terrorism.

One of the primary challenges is the coordination of efforts among different countries with varying priorities and capabilities. Each nation has unique concerns and resources, making it difficult to establish a unified approach. However, the benefits of international cooperation are manifold. By pooling resources, intelligence, and expertise, security agents can enhance their ability to detect, prevent, and respond to threats effectively.

International cooperation fosters the sharing of vital information on nuclear threats. Through robust intelligence gathering, security agencies can identify terrorist organizations' interest in dirty bombs and their plans for acquisition or production. By collaborating and sharing this intelligence, countries can collectively strengthen their defenses and develop targeted strategies to counter the specific threats posed by these organizations.

Another significant benefit of international cooperation is the establishment of comprehensive security protocols for nuclear facilities and transportation. By sharing best practices and lessons learned, security agents can develop more effective methods to detect, track, and secure nuclear materials. This collaborative approach ensures that security measures are implemented consistently across borders, limiting potential vulnerabilities that terrorists could exploit.

Cybersecurity measures are also a critical aspect of international cooperation in preventing terrorist hacking of nuclear systems. By sharing expertise and intelligence on cyber threats, countries can collectively develop robust defense mechanisms and protocols to safeguard nuclear infrastructure from cyber attacks.

Furthermore, international cooperation enables the exchange of radiation detection and monitoring strategies. By sharing research, technological advancements, and best practices, security agents can enhance their capabilities in detecting and responding to radiological threats promptly. This collaboration ensures that countries worldwide are equipped with the latest tools and knowledge to mitigate the risks associated with dirty bombs.

Emergency response plans and preparedness for dirty bomb incidents are also strengthened through international cooperation. By sharing experiences and resources, security agencies can develop comprehensive and coordinated response strategies. This collaboration ensures a swift and effective response in the event of a dirty bomb incident, minimizing the potential damage and impact on public safety.

In addition to these practical benefits, international cooperation also allows for the development of legal frameworks and penalties for individuals involved in dirty bomb activities. By aligning legal systems and penalties across borders, nations can ensure that terrorists and their accomplices face severe consequences for their actions, deterring potential threats.

Lastly, international cooperation facilitates research and development of advanced technologies to enhance dirty bomb prevention efforts. By pooling resources and expertise, countries can accelerate the development of innovative technologies that improve detection, tracking, and prevention capabilities.

In conclusion, the challenges of international cooperation in the fight against nuclear terrorism are significant, but the benefits outweigh them. Through collaboration, security agents can enhance their ability to detect, prevent, and respond to dirty bomb threats effectively. By sharing intelligence, best practices, and resources, nations can collectively strengthen their defenses, develop comprehensive security protocols, improve emergency response plans, and deter potential threats. International cooperation is an essential tool in the fight against nuclear terrorism, ensuring the safety and security of nations worldwide.

Chapter 8: Emergency Response Plans and Preparedness for Dirty Bomb Incidents

Developing Effective Emergency Response Plans

Emergency response plans are crucial in ensuring the preparedness and effectiveness of security agents in dealing with the threat of dirty bombs. In this subchapter, we will explore the key elements involved in developing such plans and the importance of coordination and cooperation among various stakeholders.

First and foremost, emergency response plans should be tailored to the specific needs and vulnerabilities of each location or nuclear facility. This requires a thorough understanding of the potential risks and the impact that a dirty bomb incident could have on the surrounding areas. Security agents must work closely with experts in nuclear materials detection and tracking technologies to assess the potential threats and develop strategies to mitigate them.

Effective security protocols for nuclear facilities and transportation are also essential in preventing terrorists from gaining access to radioactive materials. These protocols should include stringent access control measures, regular inspections, and the use of advanced technologies for detecting and preventing unauthorized entry. Additionally, cybersecurity measures must be in place to prevent terrorist hacking of nuclear systems, which could lead to the theft or sabotage of radioactive materials.

Radiation detection and monitoring strategies play a crucial role in identifying the presence of a dirty bomb and assessing the extent of the contamination. Security agents should be equipped with state-of-the-art detection devices and trained to quickly and accurately interpret the results. Regular drills and exercises should be conducted to ensure the readiness of security personnel in responding to such incidents.

Intelligence gathering on terrorist organizations' interest in dirty bombs is vital in preventing their development and use. Close collaboration with intelligence agencies and international partners is necessary to share information and stay ahead of evolving threats. International cooperation and information sharing on nuclear threats are essential in addressing the global nature of this issue and ensuring a coordinated response.

Emergency response plans should also include strategies for public awareness campaigns on the dangers of dirty bombs. Educating the public about the risks and promoting vigilance can help in preventing attacks and minimizing panic in the event of an incident.

Furthermore, legal frameworks and penalties for individuals involved in dirty bomb activities need to be in place to deter potential perpetrators. Strict enforcement of these laws will help to disrupt terrorist networks and hold those responsible accountable.

Finally, continuous research and development of advanced technologies are essential in enhancing dirty bomb prevention efforts. Investing in innovative solutions for nuclear security will enable security agents to stay ahead of terrorists and effectively mitigate the threats they pose.

In conclusion, developing effective emergency response plans is crucial in addressing the threat of dirty bombs. By focusing on nuclear materials detection and tracking technologies, security protocols, cybersecurity measures, radiation detection and monitoring strategies, intelligence gathering, international cooperation, public awareness campaigns, legal frameworks, and research and development, security agents can significantly enhance their preparedness and response capabilities in preventing and mitigating dirty bomb incidents.

Coordination between Law Enforcement and Emergency Services

In the fight against the threat of a dirty bomb, coordination between law enforcement and emergency services plays a pivotal role. The seamless integration of these two entities is crucial for effective prevention, response, and mitigation efforts. This subchapter explores the significance of this coordination and the strategies employed to ensure a robust security framework.

Law enforcement agencies and emergency services possess distinct yet complementary roles in responding to a dirty bomb incident. While law enforcement focuses on investigation, intelligence gathering, and apprehending the perpetrators, emergency services are responsible for managing the immediate aftermath, including medical response, evacuations, and containment of radiation.

To facilitate coordination, collaborative frameworks and information-sharing protocols must be established. The Department of Homeland Security (DHS) has played a pivotal role in fostering such cooperation through various initiatives. These efforts include joint training exercises, task forces, and fusion centers, where law enforcement and emergency responders can share intelligence, strategies, and best practices.

Another critical aspect of coordination is the development of comprehensive emergency response plans. These plans outline the roles and responsibilities of both law enforcement and emergency services in the event of a dirty bomb incident. Regular drills and exercises should be conducted to test the effectiveness of these plans and identify areas for improvement.

Furthermore, coordination efforts must extend beyond national borders. The international community must work together to combat the threat of dirty bombs, sharing intelligence on terrorist organizations' interest in such weapons and collaborating on prevention and response strategies. International partnerships can enhance the ability to track and intercept illicit nuclear materials, ensuring a global effort to prevent the making of dirty bombs.

Public awareness campaigns are also essential to enlist the support of the general population in identifying and reporting suspicious activities. By educating the public about the dangers of dirty bombs and the importance of reporting any potential threats, law enforcement and emergency services can benefit from the extra eyes and ears of the community.

Finally, legal frameworks and penalties must be in place to deter and punish individuals involved in dirty bomb activities. Strict laws and severe punishments serve as a deterrent and reinforce the seriousness of engaging in such malicious acts.

In conclusion, coordination between law enforcement and emergency services is vital in combating the threat of dirty bombs. Through collaborative frameworks, comprehensive emergency response plans, international cooperation, public awareness campaigns, and robust legal frameworks, security agents can work together to prevent the making of dirty bombs and enhance overall homeland security. Continuous research and development of advanced technologies further strengthen prevention efforts, providing security agents with the tools they need to stay one step ahead of potential threats.

Training and Drills to Enhance Preparedness

In the ever-evolving landscape of global security threats, it is crucial for security agents to be prepared for any potential danger. This subchapter explores the various training and drills that can help enhance preparedness in the face of the potential making of a dirty bomb and the Department of Homeland Security's efforts to stop it. These training programs are designed to equip security agents with the necessary skills and knowledge to effectively counteract the threats posed by terrorists seeking to create a dirty bomb.

One of the key components of training and drills is the use of realistic scenarios. By simulating potential dirty bomb incidents, security agents can gain firsthand experience in handling such situations. These drills involve the coordination of multiple agencies, such as law enforcement, emergency response teams, and nuclear facility personnel, to ensure a seamless and effective response in the event of an actual incident.

Furthermore, training programs focus on the utilization of nuclear materials detection and tracking technologies. Security agents are trained on the latest advancements in this field to ensure the timely identification and interception of any suspicious materials. Additionally, protocols for securing nuclear facilities and transportation are emphasized to prevent unauthorized access and ensure the safe handling of nuclear materials.

In today's digital age, cybersecurity measures play a crucial role in preventing terrorist hacking of nuclear systems. Training programs equip security agents with the necessary skills to identify and thwart cyber threats, ensuring the integrity and confidentiality of nuclear systems.

Radiation detection and monitoring strategies are also an integral part of training and drills. Security agents are trained on the proper use of radiation detection equipment, enabling them to swiftly identify and respond to any potential radiological threats.

Intelligence gathering on terrorist organizations' interest in dirty bombs is another vital aspect of training. Security agents are briefed on the latest intelligence reports and techniques for gathering information on potential threats. International cooperation and information sharing on nuclear threats is also emphasized to ensure a coordinated global response.

Emergency response plans and preparedness for dirty bomb incidents are extensively covered in training programs. Security agents are trained on the proper protocols and procedures to minimize casualties and contain the impact of a dirty bomb detonation. Public awareness campaigns are also undertaken to educate the general public on the dangers of dirty bombs and how to respond in the event of an incident.

Legal frameworks and penalties for individuals involved in dirty bomb activities are highlighted to deter potential perpetrators. Finally, research and development of advanced technologies to enhance dirty bomb prevention efforts are ongoing, and security agents are updated on the latest advancements in this field.

In conclusion, training and drills play a vital role in enhancing preparedness for the making of a dirty bomb and the Department of Homeland Security's efforts to prevent it. By equipping security agents with the necessary skills, knowledge, and technologies, we can ensure a robust response to this grave threat and safeguard the lives and security of our nation and its citizens.

Chapter 9: Public Awareness Campaigns on the Dangers of Dirty Bombs

Importance of Public Awareness in Counterterrorism

The importance of public awareness in counterterrorism cannot be overstated. In the fight against terrorism, it is crucial to involve the general public and raise awareness about the threats posed by dirty bombs. This subchapter delves into the significance of public awareness campaigns and their role in preventing the making of a dirty bomb, as well as the efforts made by the Department of Homeland Security (DHS) in this regard.

Public awareness campaigns are instrumental in educating the masses about the dangers of dirty bombs. By disseminating information about the devastating consequences of these weapons, the public can better understand the urgency of counterterrorism measures. Security agents play a vital role in implementing these campaigns, as they are on the front lines of defense and can effectively communicate the risks associated with dirty bombs.

The DHS has been at the forefront of such awareness initiatives, working tirelessly to engage both the public and relevant stakeholders. Through media campaigns, public service announcements, and outreach programs, the DHS aims to empower individuals with knowledge about the threat landscape and the necessary measures to thwart terrorist activities. By fostering a sense of responsibility and vigilance among the public, the DHS endeavors to create a proactive environment that hinders the making of a dirty bomb.

Moreover, public awareness campaigns also serve to garner support for the security protocols in place for nuclear facilities and transportation. By highlighting the stringent measures taken to safeguard nuclear materials, these campaigns alleviate concerns and build trust in the system. This, in turn, encourages public cooperation and reporting of suspicious activities, leading to enhanced security and prevention of dirty bomb incidents.

In addition, public awareness campaigns foster a culture of resilience and preparedness. By educating individuals on emergency response plans and procedures, the public can actively participate in mitigating the consequences of a dirty bomb incident. Awareness about radiation detection and monitoring strategies equips individuals to safeguard themselves and others in the event of an attack.

To ensure the success of public awareness campaigns, international cooperation and information sharing are imperative. The exchange of knowledge, best practices, and intelligence on nuclear threats between countries facilitates a comprehensive and unified approach to counterterrorism. Collaboration with international partners strengthens public awareness efforts and enhances the global fight against dirty bomb proliferation.

In conclusion, public awareness plays a critical role in counterterrorism efforts, specifically in preventing the making of a dirty bomb. By engaging security agents and the public, the DHS and other relevant authorities can effectively educate individuals about the dangers of these weapons, encourage cooperation, and build a resilient society. Through international cooperation, information sharing, and the development of advanced technologies, the fight against dirty bombs can be intensified, ensuring the safety and security of nations worldwide.

Strategies for Educating the Public about Dirty Bombs

The threat of dirty bombs is a growing concern in today's world, and it is crucial that the public is well-informed about the dangers they pose. In this subchapter, we will explore various strategies for educating the public about dirty bombs and their potential consequences. By disseminating knowledge and raising awareness, we can empower individuals to play an active role in preventing such acts of terrorism.

1. Public Awareness Campaigns: Developing and implementing comprehensive public awareness campaigns is essential. These campaigns should focus on educating the general public about the nature of dirty bombs, their potential impact on human health and the environment, and the importance of reporting any suspicious activities.

2. Collaborative Efforts: Collaboration between government agencies, law enforcement, and private organizations is crucial. By working together, we can pool resources and expertise to create targeted educational programs that effectively reach the public.

3. Use of Various Communication Channels: Utilize a range of communication channels to reach a diverse audience. This includes traditional media outlets such as television, radio, and newspapers, as well as digital platforms like social media, websites, and mobile applications.

4. Engage Community Leaders: Engaging community leaders and influential individuals can help in disseminating information effectively. By collaborating with religious leaders, community organizations, and local influencers, we can reach a broader audience and encourage them to spread the message within their respective communities.

5. School Programs: Integrate education about dirty bombs into school curricula. This will ensure that young people are educated about the threat and understand the importance of reporting any suspicious activities.

6. Public Events and Workshops: Organize public events, workshops, and seminars to provide an opportunity for experts to share information

on dirty bombs with the public. These events can also facilitate open discussions and address any concerns or misconceptions.

7. Public-Private Partnerships: Foster collaborations with private organizations, such as media outlets and technology companies, to amplify the reach of educational campaigns. This can involve the creation of public service announcements, articles, and online resources.

8. Crisis Communication Plans: Develop comprehensive crisis communication plans that provide clear and concise information to the public in the event of a dirty bomb incident. This includes guidance on evacuation procedures, sheltering in place, and other necessary safety measures.

9. Continuous Updates: Regularly update educational materials and campaigns to reflect the latest information and developments in the field. This ensures that the public remains well-informed and aware of any emerging threats.

Educating the public about dirty bombs is a shared responsibility. By employing these strategies, we can enhance public awareness, encourage reporting of suspicious activities, and ultimately contribute to the prevention of dirty bomb incidents. Continued efforts in education, collaboration, and communication are vital in our collective fight against this threat to national security.

Engaging Communities in Reporting Suspicious Activities

In the fight against the making of a dirty bomb, it is crucial to engage communities in reporting suspicious activities. Security agents play a vital role in this process, as they are at the forefront of identifying potential threats and safeguarding our nation's security. By encouraging community involvement and awareness, we can strengthen our defenses and prevent catastrophic events.

One of the primary challenges in preventing the making of a dirty bomb is the ability to gather timely and accurate intelligence. Security agents cannot be everywhere at once, which is why community engagement becomes essential. By fostering a culture of reporting suspicious activities, we create an extensive network of eyes and ears that can help identify potential threats.

To achieve this, security agents must build trust and establish strong relationships with communities. Regular outreach programs, public forums, and educational campaigns can be effective tools in raising awareness about the dangers of dirty bombs and the importance of reporting suspicious activities. By openly discussing these issues, we can empower individuals to become active participants in maintaining national security.

In addition to awareness campaigns, leveraging technology can greatly enhance community engagement. Mobile applications, dedicated hotlines, and online reporting platforms can provide a convenient and confidential way for individuals to share their concerns. Anonymity should be emphasized to encourage people who fear retaliation or backlash.

Once reports are received, it is essential to have a robust system in place to evaluate and investigate each case promptly. Security agents should collaborate with local law enforcement agencies and intelligence organizations to ensure a coordinated response. Regular training sessions can also be conducted to educate security agents on the indicators of suspicious activities and the appropriate protocols to follow.

Engaging communities in reporting suspicious activities is not only about prevention but also about building resilience. By involving the public in the fight against dirty bombs, we create a sense of ownership and shared responsibility. This collective effort will enable security agents to gather critical information, respond swiftly to potential threats, and ultimately, deter terrorists from pursuing their sinister goals.

In conclusion, engaging communities in reporting suspicious activities is a crucial aspect of preventing the making of a dirty bomb. By fostering trust, raising awareness, and leveraging technology, security agents can tap into the collective knowledge and vigilance of the public. This collaboration will strengthen our nation's security and ensure the safety of our communities.

Chapter 10: Legal Frameworks and Penalties for Individuals Involved in Dirty Bomb Activities

Legislative Measures to Combat Dirty Bomb Threats

The threat of a dirty bomb, a conventional explosive combined with radioactive material, poses a significant danger to national security and public safety. In response, legislative measures have been enacted to combat and prevent such threats. This subchapter explores the various legislative measures implemented to safeguard against dirty bomb incidents and protect the public from potential harm.

One key legislative measure is the establishment of comprehensive security protocols for nuclear facilities and transportation. These protocols ensure that proper security measures are in place at all stages of the nuclear fuel cycle, from production to disposal. They also require stringent background checks and training for personnel working in these facilities, reducing the risk of insider threats.

Furthermore, cybersecurity measures have been implemented to prevent terrorist hacking of nuclear systems. The Department of Homeland Security has collaborated with various agencies and organizations to develop robust cybersecurity strategies, including advanced encryption methods and intrusion detection systems. These measures aim to protect critical nuclear infrastructure from cyberattacks and unauthorized access.

In addition, legislative efforts have focused on enhancing radiation detection and monitoring strategies. This includes the deployment of advanced detection technologies at ports, borders, and other high-risk areas. These measures aim to identify and intercept any illicit trafficking of radioactive materials, providing an early warning system against potential dirty bomb threats.

Intelligence gathering on terrorist organizations' interest in dirty bombs plays a crucial role in prevention efforts. Legislation has been enacted to enhance information sharing and international cooperation in this regard. Intelligence agencies collaborate with their counterparts worldwide to gather and analyze intelligence on terrorist activities, ensuring early detection of any potential threats involving dirty bombs.

Emergency response plans and preparedness for dirty bomb incidents are also integral to combating this threat. Legislation mandates the development and regular updating of comprehensive response plans at the national, state, and local levels. These plans outline specific procedures for emergency response, evacuation, and decontamination, ensuring a coordinated and effective response in the event of a dirty bomb incident.

Public awareness campaigns on the dangers of dirty bombs have been instrumental in promoting vigilance and encouraging public cooperation. Legislation supports the development of educational materials and outreach programs to inform the public about the potential consequences of a dirty bomb attack. This heightens public awareness and encourages the reporting of suspicious activities or materials.

Finally, legal frameworks and penalties have been established for individuals involved in dirty bomb activities. Legislation ensures that those who engage in the production, acquisition, or use of a dirty bomb face severe legal consequences. These penalties act as a deterrent and provide law enforcement agencies with the necessary tools to prosecute those involved in these activities effectively.

To further strengthen prevention efforts, ongoing research and development of advanced technologies are being pursued. Legislation supports research initiatives aimed at enhancing dirty bomb prevention, detection, and response capabilities. This includes the development of innovative technologies, such as improved radiation detection devices, advanced modeling and simulation tools, and more effective decontamination methods.

In conclusion, legislative measures play a vital role in combating the threat of dirty bombs. Through the establishment of security protocols, cybersecurity measures, radiation detection strategies, intelligence gathering, international cooperation, emergency response plans, public awareness campaigns, legal frameworks, and research and development efforts, security agents can work together to prevent and mitigate the risks associated with dirty bomb incidents. These legislative measures reinforce the Department of Homeland Security's commitment to ensuring the safety and security of the nation and its citizens.

Prosecution and Sentencing of Individuals Involved in Dirty Bomb Activities

In the fight against the looming threat of dirty bombs, the prosecution and sentencing of individuals involved in such activities become vital components of our security efforts. This subchapter delves into the legal frameworks and penalties put in place to ensure that those responsible for these heinous acts are held accountable for their actions.

The Department of Homeland Security, in collaboration with various law enforcement agencies, has taken significant steps to develop comprehensive legal strategies to combat the production and use of dirty bombs. Prosecution of individuals involved in these activities is a crucial aspect of these strategies, aimed at deterring potential perpetrators and ensuring justice is served.

To effectively prosecute and sentence individuals involved in dirty bomb activities, it is imperative to have a robust legal framework in place. This framework includes stringent laws that classify dirty bomb activities as severe offenses, punishable by severe penalties. These penalties may range from lengthy imprisonment to significant fines, depending on the severity of the offense and the intent of the individual involved.

Additionally, the legal framework encompasses provisions for investigating and gathering evidence against individuals suspected of dirty bomb activities. This involves utilizing advanced technologies and intelligence gathering techniques to track and gather substantial evidence to support the prosecution's case.

Furthermore, international cooperation and information sharing play a crucial role in the successful prosecution and sentencing of individuals involved in dirty bomb activities. Through collaboration with other nations, law enforcement agencies can exchange intelligence, share best practices, and enhance their capabilities to identify and apprehend those involved in the production or use of dirty bombs.

The subchapter also highlights the importance of public awareness campaigns on the dangers of dirty bombs. By educating the public, security agents can gather valuable information and gain the support of citizens in reporting suspicious activities, thereby aiding in the prosecution of individuals involved in such activities.

In conclusion, the prosecution and sentencing of individuals involved in dirty bomb activities form a critical part of our comprehensive security efforts. By implementing stringent legal frameworks, collaborating internationally, and raising public awareness, security agents can effectively deter potential perpetrators, gather evidence, and ensure that justice is served. It is through these collective efforts that we can safeguard our nation and protect it from the catastrophic consequences of dirty bombs.

International Efforts to Strengthen Legal Frameworks

In the global fight against terrorism and the proliferation of nuclear materials, international cooperation and the strengthening of legal frameworks play a crucial role. Recognizing the gravity of the threat posed by the making of dirty bombs, efforts have been made to enhance existing legal frameworks and establish new ones to combat this menace. This subchapter explores the international efforts undertaken to strengthen legal frameworks and prevent the making of dirty bombs.

International cooperation and information sharing have become vital components of countering the dirty bomb threat. Various organizations, such as the International Atomic Energy Agency (IAEA) and Interpol, have been actively involved in facilitating information exchange among nations. These platforms enable security agents to gather intelligence on terrorist organizations' interest in dirty bombs, their activities, and their network.

Moreover, international conventions and treaties have been established to address the legal aspects of dirty bomb activities. The United Nations Security Council Resolution 1540, for instance, imposes binding regulations on all nations to prevent non-state actors from acquiring or using nuclear materials for malicious purposes. This resolution has been instrumental in creating legal obligations for states to enhance their domestic legal frameworks against the making of dirty bombs.

Additionally, efforts have been made to develop comprehensive emergency response plans and preparedness strategies. International organizations, such as the World Health Organization (WHO) and the International Civil Aviation Organization (ICAO), have collaborated with national governments to establish guidelines and protocols for responding to dirty bomb incidents. These initiatives aim to minimize the potential damage and ensure effective coordination among different stakeholders in emergency situations.

To deter individuals involved in dirty bomb activities, legal frameworks have been strengthened with stringent penalties. Nations have enacted legislation that imposes severe punishments on those engaged in the procurement, possession, or use of nuclear materials for illicit purposes. These penalties act as a deterrent and send a strong message that such activities will not be tolerated.

Furthermore, research and development efforts have focused on advancing technologies to enhance dirty bomb prevention. Through collaboration among governments, academia, and industry experts, innovative solutions are being explored to improve nuclear materials detection and tracking technologies, cybersecurity measures, radiation detection and monitoring strategies, and security protocols for nuclear facilities and transportation.

In conclusion, international efforts to strengthen legal frameworks are crucial in preventing the making of dirty bombs. Through international cooperation, information sharing, the establishment of treaties and conventions, the development of emergency response plans, and the enactment of stringent penalties, security agents are better equipped to combat this threat. Furthermore, ongoing research and development initiatives contribute to the enhancement of advanced technologies, which further bolster prevention efforts. It is imperative that these international efforts continue to evolve and adapt to the evolving tactics employed by terrorists, ensuring the safety and security of nations worldwide.

Chapter 11: Research and Development of Advanced Technologies to Enhance Dirty Bomb Prevention Efforts

Innovations in Preventing Dirty Bomb Attacks

Introduction:

In recent years, the threat of dirty bomb attacks has been a growing concern for security agents worldwide. The potential for devastating consequences and widespread panic makes it crucial to stay ahead of terrorists seeking to acquire and utilize nuclear materials. This subchapter explores the various innovations and strategies employed by the Department of Homeland Security (DHS) and international partners to prevent dirty bomb attacks.

Nuclear Materials Detection and Tracking Technologies:

The DHS has invested significantly in the development of advanced technologies for nuclear materials detection and tracking. These cutting-edge systems utilize state-of-the-art sensors, artificial intelligence, and machine learning algorithms to identify and locate potential threats. From handheld radiation detectors to sophisticated portal monitors, these innovations enhance security agents' ability to intercept illicit nuclear materials.

Security Protocols for Nuclear Facilities and Transportation:

The DHS has implemented stringent security protocols for nuclear facilities and transportation, ensuring a robust defense against potential attacks. These protocols include the use of advanced access control systems, radiation monitoring devices, and comprehensive background checks for personnel. The integration of biometric technologies and secure communication networks further fortifies these facilities against unauthorized access.

Cybersecurity Measures to Prevent Terrorist Hacking of Nuclear Systems:

Recognizing the evolving threat landscape, the DHS has prioritized cybersecurity measures to prevent terrorist hacking of nuclear systems. This has involved the establishment of dedicated teams to identify vulnerabilities, conduct regular penetration testing, and develop robust encryption protocols. Collaborative efforts with the intelligence community and private sector partners have strengthened cybersecurity defenses and minimized the risk of unauthorized access to critical nuclear infrastructure.

Radiation Detection and Monitoring Strategies:

To effectively counter dirty bomb threats, security agents have adopted innovative radiation detection and monitoring strategies. These include the deployment of mobile radiation detection units, aerial surveillance systems, and the integration of real-time data analysis. By leveraging these strategies, security agents can quickly identify suspicious radiation signatures, track potential threats, and respond swiftly to mitigate the risk of an attack.

Intelligence Gathering on Terrorist Organizations' Interest in Dirty Bombs:

Understanding the intentions and capabilities of terrorist organizations is paramount in preventing dirty bomb attacks. The DHS, along with international partners, has significantly enhanced intelligence gathering efforts to monitor and assess threats. Through improved information sharing and collaboration, security agents can identify emerging trends, track procurement networks, and disrupt potential plots before they materialize.

International Cooperation and Information Sharing on Nuclear Threats:

Recognizing that nuclear threats transcend national borders, the DHS actively engages in international cooperation and information sharing. This comprehensive approach allows for the exchange of intelligence, best practices, and collaborative efforts to prevent dirty bomb attacks. By fostering strong relationships with international partners, security agents can collectively enhance their ability to detect, track, and deter nuclear threats.

Conclusion:

Preventing dirty bomb attacks requires constant innovation and collaboration among security agents and international partners. The DHS's efforts encompass cutting-edge technologies, robust security protocols, cybersecurity measures, intelligence gathering, and public awareness campaigns. By continuously evolving and refining these strategies, security agents can stay one step ahead of terrorists, safeguarding our nations from the devastating consequences of a dirty bomb attack.

Investing in Research and Development for Enhanced Security

In the ever-evolving world of security threats, it is imperative for security agents to stay one step ahead of terrorists and their destructive plans. The making of a dirty bomb is a haunting reality that poses a significant risk to national and global security. To combat this threat, the Department of Homeland Security has recognized the need to invest in research and development (R&D) initiatives to enhance security measures.

One key area of focus is the development of nuclear materials detection and tracking technologies. By investing in cutting-edge technologies, security agents can effectively identify and locate radioactive materials, preventing terrorists from obtaining them for sinister purposes. These advancements enable swift action and apprehension of those involved in illicit activities.

Security protocols for nuclear facilities and transportation are also crucial in mitigating the threat of dirty bombs. R&D efforts should focus on creating robust security systems that protect nuclear facilities from unauthorized access and ensure the safe transportation of nuclear materials. By continuously improving these protocols, security agents can minimize vulnerabilities and enhance overall safety.

In the digital age, cybersecurity measures play a vital role in preventing terrorist hacking of nuclear systems. R&D efforts should concentrate on developing advanced cybersecurity technologies that safeguard critical infrastructure from cyber threats. By fortifying these systems, security agents can prevent unauthorized access and manipulations that could lead to a dirty bomb incident.

Radiation detection and monitoring strategies are essential in detecting the presence of radioactive materials. R&D should aim to enhance the accuracy and efficiency of radiation detection devices, enabling security agents to identify potential threats swiftly. Additionally, developing portable and affordable monitoring tools will empower law enforcement agencies to conduct comprehensive checks in various environments.

Intelligence gathering on terrorist organizations' interest in dirty bombs is essential to preempt potential attacks. By investing in advanced intelligence technologies, security agents can gather critical information on terrorist networks, their intentions, and their capabilities. This knowledge will enable proactive measures and targeted interventions to disrupt their plans.

International cooperation and information sharing on nuclear threats are paramount in combating the global menace of dirty bombs. R&D efforts should focus on developing platforms and protocols that facilitate seamless information exchange between countries. By sharing intelligence, best practices, and technological advancements, security agents can collectively strengthen global security.

Emergency response plans and preparedness for dirty bomb incidents are crucial to minimize the impact of an attack. Investing in R&D initiatives that evaluate and enhance response strategies will equip security agents with the necessary tools to effectively manage and mitigate the consequences of such incidents.

Public awareness campaigns on the dangers of dirty bombs should also be a priority. R&D efforts should aim to develop comprehensive educational materials and initiatives that raise public awareness about the risks and consequences associated with dirty bombs. By educating the public, security agents can foster a sense of vigilance and encourage community involvement in preventing such attacks.

Legal frameworks and penalties for individuals involved in dirty bomb activities also play a critical role in deterring potential perpetrators. R&D efforts should focus on evaluating existing laws and regulations to ensure they are comprehensive and effective. By continuously updating legal frameworks and imposing severe penalties, security agents can create a strong deterrent against involvement in dirty bomb activities.

Finally, investing in R&D for advanced technologies is vital to enhance dirty bomb prevention efforts continually. By exploring emerging technologies, such as artificial intelligence, robotics, and quantum computing, security agents can develop innovative solutions that proactively address evolving threats. These technologies have the potential to revolutionize the field of security and provide unprecedented capabilities in preventing dirty bomb incidents.

In conclusion, investing in research and development is essential for security agents in the fight against dirty bombs. By focusing on various areas such as nuclear materials detection, cybersecurity, intelligence gathering, and public awareness, security agents can enhance their capabilities and stay ahead of terrorists' evolving tactics. Continued investment in R&D will ensure that security measures are proactive, robust, and effective in preventing the making of a dirty bomb.

Future Outlook for Advanced Technologies in Counterterrorism Efforts

The fight against terrorism has always been a top priority for security agents, especially when it comes to the making of a dirty bomb. In recent years, technological advancements have played a crucial role in enhancing counterterrorism efforts. As we look ahead, the future outlook for advanced technologies in this field is promising, offering new tools and strategies to safeguard against the threat of dirty bombs.

One area where advanced technologies are making significant strides is in nuclear materials detection and tracking. With the development of sophisticated sensors and detectors, security agents can now identify and locate nuclear materials more rapidly and accurately. These technologies, along with improved tracking systems, enable authorities to detect any illicit movement of nuclear materials, thereby preventing their misuse.

Moreover, security protocols for nuclear facilities and transportation are continuously evolving. Advanced access control systems, biometric authentication, and surveillance technologies are being implemented to fortify the security of these critical infrastructures. Enhanced screening procedures, including advanced imaging technologies, are also being employed to detect any illicit objects or substances.

As the digital landscape becomes increasingly interconnected, cybersecurity measures are paramount to prevent terrorist hacking of nuclear systems. The future will see the development of robust encryption techniques, advanced intrusion detection systems, and artificial intelligence-based algorithms to identify and neutralize cyber threats effectively.

Radiation detection and monitoring strategies are also being revolutionized by advanced technologies. Miniaturized and portable radiation detectors, coupled with real-time monitoring systems and data analytics, enable security agents to swiftly respond to any radioactive threats and mitigate their impact on public safety.

Intelligence gathering on terrorist organizations' interest in dirty bombs remains a crucial aspect of counterterrorism efforts. Advanced data analysis techniques, including machine learning and predictive analytics, are anticipated to enhance intelligence capabilities, providing security agents with timely insights into potential threats.

Furthermore, international cooperation and information sharing on nuclear threats are vital to combat the global menace of dirty bombs. Advanced communication systems and secure information-sharing platforms will facilitate real-time collaboration between different nations, enabling efficient response and proactive prevention of such incidents.

Emergency response plans and preparedness for dirty bomb incidents will continue to be refined with the integration of advanced technologies. Simulation models and virtual reality training programs will help security agents gain practical experience in handling various scenarios, ensuring a swift and effective response during crisis situations.

To raise public awareness on the dangers of dirty bombs, impactful campaigns utilizing advanced media technologies, such as virtual reality, augmented reality, and social media platforms, will be employed. These campaigns will educate the public about the consequences of dirty bomb incidents and emphasize the importance of collective efforts in preventing such attacks.

Legal frameworks and penalties for individuals involved in dirty bomb activities will also be strengthened. Advanced forensic technologies and evidence collection methodologies will aid in the identification and prosecution of perpetrators, serving as a deterrent for potential offenders.

Finally, research and development of advanced technologies will remain a priority in enhancing dirty bomb prevention efforts. Investments in innovative technologies, such as nanotechnology, robotics, and advanced materials, will lead to the development of novel detection and prevention tools, further strengthening our defenses against this threat.

In conclusion, the future outlook for advanced technologies in counterterrorism efforts is promising. Through the development and implementation of state-of-the-art technologies, security agents will be better equipped to prevent the making of a dirty bomb and protect society from its devastating consequences. The continuous evolution of these technologies, coupled with international cooperation and public awareness, will ensure a safer and more secure future.

Conclusion: Safeguarding Against Dirty Bomb Threats - A Collective Responsibility of Security Agents

In conclusion, the threat of dirty bombs remains a significant concern for security agents worldwide. The making of a dirty bomb poses a grave danger to national security, public safety, and the global community as a whole. However, the Department of Homeland Security and various security agencies have been tirelessly working to prevent the making of dirty bombs by terrorists and protect against potential attacks.

The fight against dirty bomb threats requires a collective responsibility from security agents across various sectors. This subchapter has explored several key areas where security agents play a crucial role in safeguarding against dirty bomb threats.

Nuclear materials detection and tracking technologies are essential in preventing terrorists from acquiring or smuggling radioactive materials. Security agents must stay updated with the latest advancements in this field and collaborate with experts to implement effective detection and tracking systems.

Security protocols for nuclear facilities and transportation are vital to ensuring the safety and security of radioactive materials. Security agents must enforce stringent measures, including access control, surveillance, and regular inspections, to prevent any unauthorized access or potential theft.

Cybersecurity measures play a critical role in preventing terrorists from hacking into nuclear systems and gaining control over radioactive materials. Security agents must work closely with cybersecurity experts to strengthen the resilience of nuclear facilities and prevent any cyber threats.

Radiation detection and monitoring strategies are essential in identifying and containing any potential dirty bomb incidents. Security agents should be adequately trained in radiation detection techniques and equipped with the necessary tools to respond effectively to such situations.

Intelligence gathering on terrorist organizations' interest in dirty bombs is crucial to stay ahead of potential threats. Security agents must collaborate with intelligence agencies and share information to identify and disrupt any plans related to dirty bombs.

International cooperation and information sharing on nuclear threats are vital in preventing the proliferation of dirty bombs. Security agents must actively engage in international forums, share intelligence, and collaborate with other countries to strengthen global security against dirty bomb threats.

Emergency response plans and preparedness for dirty bomb incidents are essential to minimize the impact of an attack. Security agents should participate in regular drills, coordinate with local authorities, and ensure effective communication channels to respond swiftly and efficiently in case of an incident.

Public awareness campaigns on the dangers of dirty bombs are essential to educate and engage the public in the fight against terrorism. Security agents must actively participate in these campaigns, providing accurate information and empowering individuals to report any suspicious activities.

Legal frameworks and penalties for individuals involved in dirty bomb activities play a crucial role in deterring potential perpetrators. Security agents must work closely with legal authorities to ensure strict enforcement of laws and regulations related to dirty bomb activities.

Research and development of advanced technologies are essential in enhancing dirty bomb prevention efforts. Security agents should actively support and participate in research initiatives to develop innovative solutions and technologies to counter the evolving threats.

In conclusion, safeguarding against dirty bomb threats is a collective responsibility of security agents across various domains. By staying informed, collaborating, and actively contributing to prevention efforts, security agents can play a pivotal role in protecting nations and communities from the devastating consequences of dirty bomb attacks. Together, we can build a safer and more secure future.